THE IMPORTANCE
of
TITHES
and
OFFERINGS

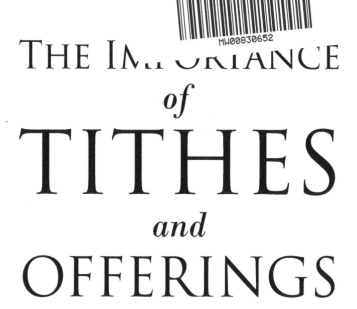

Honour the LORD with thy substance, and with the firstfruits of all thine increase: So shall thy barns be filled with plenty, and thy presses shall burst out with new wine. (Proverbs 3:9–10, kjv)

Jacqui D. Williams

THE IMPORTANCE
of
TITHES
and
OFFERINGS

Jacqui D. Williams

Christian Faith
PUBLISHING

ISBN 978-1-0980-4954-6 (paperback)
ISBN 978-1-0980-4955-3 (digital)

Christian Faith Publishing, Inc.
832 Park Avenue
Meadville, PA 16335
www.christianfaithpublishing.com

All scriptures are taken from the KING JAMES VERSION (KJV): KING JAMES VERSION, public domain.

Printed in the United States of America

TABLE OF CONTENTS

CHAPTER 1

Understanding the Basics of Tithes and Offerings

The way we manage our finances reveals who and what we place as a priority. Matthew 6:21 tells us that where our treasure lies, our heart will be there also. God looks at the condition and intentions of our heart, and He can see if we are keeping Him first just by the way we handle our money. Money can be one of many instruments used to expose the attitude of our heart, and when we freely sow our tithes and offerings, this act of love toward God shows our willingness to honor Him with the first fruits of all our increase.

It is clear that God doesn't need our money, and I am pretty sure there are no financial exchanges made in heaven. However, through the ages, whether in the forms of currency, herds of cattle or flocks of sheep, giving of tithes and offerings has been demonstrated throughout the Old and New Testaments to present day. Time has shown that when we obey God's law and order, the blessings of God will follow; this is not magic, but what He has set in place. Just like the law of gravity, if you step off a cliff or a high-rise building, it is not magic that you fall to the ground, it just happens because that's how the law of gravity works. In *Luke 6:38, kjv;* God says, *"Give, and it shall be given unto you; good measure, pressed down, and shaken together, and running over, shall men give into your bosom."* This isn't magic, but one of the many promises of God at work.

> *This book of the law shall not depart out of thy mouth; but thou shalt meditate therein day and night, that thou mayest observe to do according to all that is written therein: for then thou shalt make thy way prosperous, and then thou shalt have good success. (Joshua 1:8, kjv)*

When we give, we should not give grudgingly nor just to receive the blessings of God, but give out of a pure and loving heart towards God. Therefore, the blessings are then a result of our obedience to God; as stated in *Luke 11:28 kjv;* *"But he said, Yea rather, blessed are they that hear the word of God, and keep it."* But giving with no purpose of love or honor for God, makes our giving as nothing. In *1 Corinthians 13:3, kjv;* it states, *"And though I bestow all my goods to feed the poor, and though I give my body to be burned, and have not charity, it profiteth me nothing."*

Let every man decide in his own heart what he will give, and it is a good practice to work out what your tithe will be before you take care of anything else. I know for me, I sow my tithe and offerings before I pay any bills, set aside a savings, or before I buy something special. My tithe and offerings are determined first, this way I don't get off course by putting other things before God. So, what is considered the tithe? The tithe definition from the dictionary version means one-tenth of annual produce or earnings and the offering is anything after the tithe that we decide to give from the free will of our heart.

Every man according as he purposeth in his heart, so let him give; not grudgingly, or of necessity: for God loveth a cheerful giver. (2 Corinthians 9:7, kjv)

And as soon as the commandment came abroad, the children of Israel brought in abundance the firstfruits of corn, wine, and oil, and honey, and of all the increase of the field; and the tithe of all things brought they in abundantly. (2 Chronicles 31:5, kjv)

And concerning the tithe of the herd, or of the flock, even of whatsoever passeth under the rod, the tenth shall be holy unto the Lord. (Leviticus 27:32, kjv)

I grew up watching my mother sow her tithes and offerings every week at our family church, and I was waiting for the time when I could do the same. But the actual reality was, I could have done the same even at that young age. I remember asking my mother, "how do I go about sowing my tithes?" She told me once I am older and start working, I can begin to sow a tenth of my salary, and this would be my tithe; so what you are giving now from your allowances is an offering.

Later, I learned more about this in better detail as I got older, that whether you are working or not you can still sow your tithes with the 10 percent of any money you receive. Meaning, when I was young and receiving an allowance from my father, that was increase to me; therefore, whatever amount that was I could give a tenth of that amount and sow it as my tithe. My mother was always willing to teach me in every way she could as it related to my relationship with God. Later we learned more as we studied and listened to teachings from God's word, that tithing is also applied from any extra money you may receive. You may think like we did, that tithing is only from your regular paycheck, and when it comes to extra outside money you don't have to include it. But it's not that way at all, the word of God says, to "Honour the LORD with thy substance, and with the first-fruits of all thine increase:" (Proverbs 3:9, kjv). As I grew in the word and later learned that no matter what money I received, I could take 10 percent and sow it as my tithe.

Once I started working at age nineteen, I was so excited to start sowing my tithes, and after doing this for a while, I later learned from my older sister Jan, the importance of offerings. In *Malachi 3:8, kjv*; God says, *"Will a man rob God? Yet ye have robbed me. But ye say, Wherein have we robbed thee? In tithes and offerings."* My sister Jan and I were talking one day about tithing and she mentioned, it's not only spoken by God that we tithe, but that we give our tithe and offering to the Lord. I then began learning more and more about the importance of both, and made sure I was doing both. This was important to me because I wanted to please and honor God in every way I could. My sister and I would have good conversations about tithes and offerings, and I was always so encouraged by both my parents' and sister's heart for giving.

He that is faithful in that which is least is faithful also in much: and he that is unjust in the least is unjust also in much. (Luke 16:10, kjv)

He that hath pity upon the poor lendeth unto the Lord; and that which he hath given will he pay him again. (Proverbs 19:17, kjv)

But take diligent heed to do the commandment and the law, which Moses the servant of the Lord charged you, to love the Lord your God, and to walk in all his ways, and to keep his commandments, and to cleave unto him, and to serve him with all your heart and with all your soul. (Joshua 22:5, kjv)

Blessed are they that keep his testimonies, and that seek him with the whole heart. (Psalm 119:2, kjv)

CHAPTER 2

Pleasing God in Our Giving

A lot of times we think that it is difficult to please God because there is so much to consider in His word, and no way I can follow all the commandments and the dos and don'ts. But it is not that way at all, there are some things that may come easier for us to do and there are some things that are more challenging. For example, sowing my tithes and offerings has always been a joy to me and something I would consider easier for me to follow because it is something that I have always wanted to do because of my love for God. But when God says to love thy neighbor as thyself or to turn the other cheek when you are wronged by someone, then it becomes more difficult to be obedient to what God has said in His word. This is why I say, if we at least start by being obedient in the things that may come easier to us, then the things that are harder God will help us. God's grace is sufficient for every area of our life, and without Him we can do nothing.

And he said unto me, My grace is sufficient for thee: for my strength is made perfect in weakness. Most gladly therefore will I rather glory in my infirmities, that the power of Christ may rest upon me. (2 Corinthians 12:9, kjv)

I am the vine, ye are the branches: He that abideth in me, and I in him, the same bringeth forth much fruit: for without me ye can do nothing. (John 15:5, kjv)

In Genesis 4 from the Old Testament both Cain and Abel gave an offering to God, one was accepted and the other one rejected. Why? They both gave, but what was the difference in the giving? The only difference would be the attitude in which it was given. Always know that God can see right through our hearts and He knows already whether it is a heart of cheerfulness or a don't-care, second-best attitude. If we are going to give, God wants the first fruits (right off the top) (best of the best) of whatever we are giving. Abel killed the firstborn animal from his flock and offered it up to God. Cain offered a portion from his crop, but it was not his best and God knew it. God knows our hearts and the attitude in which we give, and He wants us to give cheerfully (be excited and happy) and not grudgingly (unwilling and unenthusiastic). We must give the best of our first fruits, and not leftovers which leaves God for last.

Cain was a farmer over the soil and crops, so it was nothing wrong with him giving from his crop, but he did not give the best of his crop. Abel was a shepherd over the sheep and he killed the firstborn of his flock. He offered to God the firstling of his top best. So the focus is not what is being given, but that which you are giving is from the first of your best. That's why when people ask the question, should I be giving from my net or from my gross, you can easily answer them and say, of course from your gross. The net is not your best, it is the leftovers after the taxes have been pulled. The gross is your top best and is considered the first before anything else is touched.

Also, when you are giving to the Lord, it should mean something to you; in short, it should cost you something. Abel's firstborn from his flock cost him something because it meant something to him. Cain's didn't mean anything, he held back the best of his crop and gave God the leftovers. Remember, the story of the widow who gave her last two mites in the offering, and Jesus said, she gave more than all who had given much from their richly abundance. Why, because Jesus knew that was all she had, and it cost her something.

Can you think back on a time when someone gave you a gift that you could tell they didn't give much thought to it at all, or you assumed it didn't cost them much of anything, not that the price should matter, but we know the saying, "It is the thought that counts," and we all know that nobody has to give us anything. But whether or not this way of giving is okay for us, I would not recommend that we operate this way with God. Thinking, "They could have kept this," I am sure God could think this same way. If it doesn't mean something to you, why should your second-best giving mean something to God.

And the king said unto Araunah, Nay; but I will surely buy it of thee at a price: neither will I offer burnt offerings unto the Lord my God of that which doth cost me nothing. So David bought the threshingfloor and the oxen for fifty shekels of silver. And David built there an altar unto the Lord, and offered burnt offerings and peace offerings. So the Lord was intreated for the land, and the plague was stayed from Israel. (2 Samuel 24:24–25, kjv)

And Jesus sat over against the treasury, and beheld how the people cast money into the treasury: and many that were rich cast in much. And there came a certain poor widow, and she threw in two mites, which make a farthing. And he called unto him his disciples, and saith unto them, Verily I say unto you, That this poor widow hath cast more in, than all they which have cast into the treasury: For all they did cast in of their abundance; but she of her want did cast in all that she had, even all her living. (Mark 12:41–44, kjv)

CHAPTER 3

Is Tithing for Believers Today?

Whether or not to sow tithes and offerings seems to have always been either a raised question or a wonder of should we or shouldn't we? Why does it always seem to be such an issue with some, who question why they have to give 10 percent of their hard-earned money, without realizing that they would not have any of it, if it were not for the Lord blessing them with the health and strength to be able to earn it in the first place. This is where the word grudgingly comes to mine, which means you are unwilling and reluctant to share or give what is all His to begin with. God loves a cheerful giver and if your giving is anything less, then I would say, just keep it. *"For where your treasure is, there will your heart be also." (Matthew 6:21, kjv)*

The fact is Jesus came not to destroy the laws, but to fulfill them. But to debate or dismiss whether or not tithes and offerings is for the believer today, does it really matter? Why can't we honor the tithe and offering practice just because we love and want to honor God this way? God speaks about giving throughout both the Old and New Testaments and how we use our money shows where our hearts' treasures lie.

Now, true if you are a born-again Christian who has sincerely received the Lord Jesus Christ as your personal Lord and Saviour, not paying your tithes and offerings will not keep you out of heaven. Absolutely not, you are sealed unto the day of redemption, these are two separate issues, your soul for all eternity, and handling of your money affects your present well-being while here on earth. However, I would think because you are a born-again Christian that out of your love for God that you would want to honor Him this way. But only you can make that decision, not me nor anyone else.

But let's look at it this way, choosing to honor God with our tithes and offerings is just another way to look at how we handle our finances, and having proper management shows that we are being a good steward over what God has entrusted into our hands. Let's not forget, sowing our tithes and offerings helps assist in the building and spreading of the Gospel for the sustaining of the Lord's house (the church). That's why God says to bring all the tithes into the Lord's storehouse, so the necessities of the body (the church) can be provided for. The Lord's storehouse is considered your local place of worship, where you are being fed the Word of God, this should be where you sow your regular tithes and offerings. That's why the practice of tithes and offerings has continued on throughout the Old and New Testaments into the present day. However, if you do not have a local church home, then anywhere else you sow, is considered an offering, not a tithe.

> *Bring ye all the tithes into the storehouse, that there may be meat in mine house, and prove me now herewith, saith the Lord of hosts, if I will not open you the windows of heaven, and pour you out a blessing, that there shall not be room enough to receive it. (Malachi 3:10, kjv)*

But this thing commanded I them, saying, Obey my voice, and I will be your God, and ye shall be my people: and walk ye in all the ways that I have commanded you, that it may be well unto you. (Jeremiah 7:23, kjv)

CHAPTER 4

The Law Fulfilled in Jesus Alone

Tithes and offerings was a law requirement in the Old Testament and was considered one of many orders put in place for the Israelites to obey, same as the Ten Commandments that was given by God to Moses to bring a standard of living for the people to follow. But once Jesus came, He did not throw away the laws, they were all fulfilled in Him. Jesus gave the ultimate sacrifice by offering His life through the shedding of His blood and being nailed to the cross, ended the need for any more slain sacrifices to get us back in right standing with God. The law is now fulfilled in Christ Jesus alone. Thank you, Jesus!

Think not that I am come to destroy the law, or the prophets:

I am not come to destroy, but to fulfil. (Matthew 5:17, kjv)

For what the law could not do, in that it was weak through the flesh, God sending his own Son in the likeness of sinful flesh, and for sin, condemned sin in the flesh: That the righteousness of the law might be fulfilled in us, who walk not after the flesh, but after the Spirit. (Romans 8:3–4, kjv)

Thou shalt have no other gods before me. Thou shalt not make unto thee any graven image, or any likeness of any thing that is in heaven above, or that is in the earth beneath, or that is in the water under the earth: Thou shalt not bow down thyself to them, nor serve them: for I the Lord thy God am a jealous God, visiting the iniquity of the fathers upon the children unto the third and fourth generation of them that hate me; And shewing mercy unto

*thousands of them that love me,
and keep my commandments.
(Exodus 20:3–6, kjv)*

So should tithes and offerings be a practice for believers today? Why not? I say, yes!
Remember, Jesus said, that He came not to do
away with the Law, but to fulfill it. In the Old
Testament, it states, that we are to love God
with all our heart, with all our soul, and with all
our strength, this is the (*first and great commandment*). In the New Testament, Jesus said, "I give
you another commandment, like unto it, to love
thy neighbor as thyself, and if you do this you
will have fulfilled all of the law. Jesus, didn't say,
that the previous commandment was abolished,
He said, I give you another one, *"And the second
is like unto it," Matthew 22:39, kjv;* meaning, in
addition to.

Now, tithing is not a law requirement for
our present day, but with the coming arrival,
death, and resurrection of Jesus Christ our Lord
and Saviour, came the fulfillment within all
the past laws which gave us as children of God
the freedom and choice to serve and worship
Him. By having this freedom do some take that
opportunity to say, tithing is not a law for us

today; therefore, I do not have to tithe. This of course is your freedom of choice which you may choose to do, and plenty have taken this route. But as I mentioned before, every individual must make their own personal decision as to how they want to honor God. But remember, God has not changed, even though people and times have. God's word worked then and works now, and His overflow of blessings are favored upon those that choose to honor and worship Him in spirit and in truth.

> *Hear, O Israel: The Lord our God is one Lord: And thou shalt love the Lord thy God with all thine heart, and with all thy soul, and with all thy might. And these words, which I command thee this day, shall be in thine heart: And thou shalt teach them diligently unto thy children, and shalt talk of them when thou sittest in thine house, and when thou walkest by the way, and when thou liest down, and when thou risest up. (Deuteronomy 6:4–7, kjv)*

Jesus said unto him, Thou shalt love the Lord thy God with all thy heart, and with all thy soul, and with all thy mind. This is the first and great commandment. And the second is like unto it, Thou shalt love thy neighbor as thyself. On these two commandments hang all the law and the prophets. (Matthew 22:37–40, kjv)

Let me also mention that the sowing of tithes and offerings into our local church should not be used as an opportunity to withdraw from as a savings account during a personal time of need. Once we give, our trust should be in God, that He will direct the leaders to use the monies sown for the good of God's people, that will take care of the needs and up keep of that particular church. If for any reason the leaders do not use the tithes and offerings from God's people as directed by God's Holy Spirit, then God will in fact deal with those leaders accordingly. Remember, God will always protect your giving whenever you give with the right heart and intentions. There are times when church leaders are guided by the Holy Spirit to sow into the lives of their local congregation (church family members), which is an awesome blessing, but this is a leader's decision based on the Spirit of God directing them to do so; not a time for us to request personal withdrawals from what we have previously sown.

> *But when thou doest alms, let not thy left hand know what thy right hand doeth: That thine alms may be in secret: and thy Father which seeth in secret himself shall reward thee openly. (Matthew 6:3–4, kjv)*

> *For if there be first a willing mind, it is accepted according to that a man hath, and not according to that he hath not. (2 Corinthians 8:12, kjv)*

CHAPTER 5

God's Grace: My Personal Story

In this chapter, I share a personal story that I hope will encourage you. In *Romans 15:4, kjv;* it states, *"For whatsoever things were written afore-time were written for our learning, that we through patience and comfort of the scriptures might have hope."* In short, this means, you can learn from what another person has gone through; or you can be encouraged for the good by witnessing another person's godly example.

Some years ago, I went through a difficult time that seriously affected my finances and as a result I was not tithing as regularly as before. I went from consistently sowing my tithes for over thirty-one years, to barely sowing at all. Meaning, sometimes I would and sometimes I wouldn't based on whether I was able to or not.

In short, what I was doing, was putting the bills before God, which made my financial situation grow increasingly worse.

It was clear to me what was happening, I was not completely trusting God through the tough times. Even though the bills were mounting, I should have continued to sow my tithes and trust God to bring me through the storm. One thing I have learned about God; is that through it all He makes a way. Even in times when we are not faithful to Him, He is faithful to us. As the months went on, I was back and forth tithing here and there for about two to three years. However, I still believed in my heart that tithing was right for me to do, I just was not doing it, which is even worse. Remember, God's word says in *James 4:17, kjv; "Therefore to him that knoweth to do good, and doeth it not, to him it is sin."* So needless to say, I was in sin and going through extremely because I knew I was not being obedient to what God had revealed to my heart.

Let's face it, we all know we have responsibilities to take care of, but I would tell anyone to trust God during those tough financial times. I know it can be tempting to use the money for other things first, but at all cost, keep God first by sowing your tithes and offerings as a priority. I am a witness that you will begin to see God do great and mighty things on your behalf whenever you keep God as a priority in your life. In Malachi 3:10, God says, to prove (test) Him and see if He will not open the windows of heaven and pour you out a blessing. This is not magic, or some sort of wand or genie operation; not at all. This is simply honoring God with a sincere heart of love and trusting Him to bring you through victoriously; and in your obedience to God's word the blessings come.

When we choose bills and other things before God, it only increases the responsibility for more bills, because you left God for last. Those of us who regularly sow our tithes and offerings know the disappointment that comes when you are not honoring God. This can happen in other ways too, not just financially. As believers whenever we fail to honor God in our life, a shadow of remorse is cast over our entire being and spirit, until we honor Him first in our life. In honoring God in any area of your life, you will see how He works all things together for your good.

And we know that all things work together for good to them that love God, to them who are the called according to his purpose. (Romans 8:28, kjv)

And he said unto me, My grace is sufficient for thee: for my strength is made perfect in weakness. Most gladly therefore will I rather glory in my infirmities, that the power of Christ may rest upon me. (2 Corinthians 12:9, kjv)

It is of the Lord's mercies that we are not consumed, because his compassions fail not. They are new every morning: great is thy faithfulness. (Lamentations 3:22–23, kjv)

After praying and trusting God for several months the doors began to open and the strenuous circumstances that I found myself in had ended and were resolved on my behalf. I knew only God could have done such marvelous exploits in my life. God showed His faithfulness to me even when I was not always faithful to Him. As the scripture mentions in Romans 2:4, it was the goodness of God that led me to repentance. I am forever grateful to God for His goodness and provision that He continues to show me every day.

> *Or despisest thou the riches of his goodness and forbearance and longsuffering; not knowing that the goodness of God leadeth thee to repentance? (Romans 2:4, kjv)*

When I made a decision to get back on track and remained consistent in sowing my tithes and offerings, not only did I have peace within myself, I knew I was doing what God had always spoke to my heart to do. I would say, my most relief from it all, came primarily because I knew I was walking in obedience, and then seeing the hand of God working through and bringing me out of that difficult storm just confirmed to me once again of God's love, mercy, and favor over my life. We should not ignore opportunities to get our life in order, but be quick to repent and change, so we may live a life that will honor God, and this will allow us to experience His best.

Sowing of my tithes and offerings is another part of my personal relationship I have with the Lord, and I take joy and pleasure in my giving to Him. I thank God that I am a witness to His goodness and provision, that He is, and I know will always continue to be the sole provider of all of my needs. God is without a doubt my Jehovah Jireh, the Lord God my Provider!

Whether you believe or not that tithing is necessary for today's Christian is left for each individual to decide. But as for me and my house I choose to honor the Lord in this way and I take extreme pleasure in giving of my tithes and offerings. I do this not because I have to, but because I want to. There is joy and freedom released within me whenever I give in any area of my life.

> *And Abraham called the name of that place Jehovah-jireh: as it is said to this day, In the mount of the Lord it shall be seen. (Genesis 22:14, kjv)*

There are several names of God referenced throughout the Old Testament. The following seven are the redemptive names of God:

1. *Jehovah Jireh: The Lord My Provider (Genesis 22:14, kjv)*
2. *Jehovah Rapha: The Lord My Healer (Exodus 15:26, kjv)*
3. *Jehovah Nissi: The Lord My Banner (Exodus 17:15, kjv)*
4. *Jehovah Shalom: The Lord My Peace (Judges 6:23–24, kjv)*
5. *Jehovah Raah: The Lord My Shepherd (Psalm 23:1, kjv)*
6. *Jehovah Tsidkenu: The Lord Our Righteousness (Jeremiah 23:6, kjv)*
7. *Jehovah Shammah: The Lord Is There (Ezekiel 48:35, kjv)*
   - *Jehovah meaning: God the Lord (Psalm 83:18, kjv)*
   - *Elohim meaning: God the Creator (Genesis 1:1, kjv)*
   - *El Shaddai meaning: God the Almighty (Genesis 17:1, kjv)*

CHAPTER 6

Work Out Your Own Salvation

In Philippians 2:12, it says, let every man *"work out your own salvation with fear and trembling"*. I would say to anyone you have to pray and spend time reading God's word and allow His Holy Spirit to speak to your heart in what He would have you to do regarding tithes and offerings. You have to decide based on your personal relationship with God how you will honor Him. This is all a part of working out your own salvation; but I will tell you this, there is liberty anytime you are free in your finances with God. God has spoken clearly to me in this area, it is a part of who I am as a believer. I share my story to hopefully encourage and help others to better understand the importance as well as the benefits of tithes and offerings.

In *Psalm 37:25, kjv;* it says, *"I have been young, and now am old; yet have I not seen the righteous forsaken, nor his seed begging bread."* Through my many years as a believer, God has provided in so many ways. At times, I may have wondered just how God was going to come through, but yet, I always knew He would. I knew that somehow or someway, He would use somebody's power, ability, and influence on my behalf. I thank God for those tough times; not because I enjoyed it. But because it was awesome seeing God's mighty hand pull me through. This allowed me to witness and experience once again the excellence of who He is.

> *And I will rebuke the devourer for your sakes, and he shall not destroy the fruits of your ground; neither shall your vine cast her fruit before the time in the field, saith the Lord of hosts. And all nations shall call you blessed: for ye shall be a delightsome land, saith the Lord of hosts. (Malachi 3:11–12, kjv)*

We all should be able to look back over our life and tell a story of God's goodness and favor that has brought us through a tough time. It doesn't have to be financial, there are countless other ways we have been a witness to His love, favor, and goodness in our lives.

Open up your heart and allow the Holy Spirit of God to reveal God's love for you, and while you are receiving His love for you, meditate on your love for Him. I believe when you have a heart of love for anyone that increases your desire to want to give to them. A key indicator to check when someone says they love you, is if they have a heart to give to you. Saying just "I Love You" can be an empty phrase if it is not followed up and shown with actions. Remember, faith without works is dead, and I would say, if your love is not demonstrated through actions, then that love is null and void. So examine your love for God, and pray that He will help free you in the area of financial giving.

Let's be real with ourselves, all that we are, all that we have, and all that we enjoy such as our life, family, friends, money, homes, cars, jobs, etc., are all gifts that God has entrusted into our hands. We need to remember we are not owners, only stewards over what God has allowed us to enjoy while here on earth. He wants us to use and handle each wisely and does not want it nor them to have us. Once you can't give it back or release it when God asks, then it or them has you. Giving 10 percent is a mere pittance to ask of us in the big scheme of things, knowing that it is all His to begin with. The tithe is only the beginning, the overflow of blessings comes in the giving of the offerings. It almost seems out of order to talk about giving of offerings, if you have not yet gotten to the point where you can give the tithe. Remember, in Malachi 3:8, God says, you have robbed me of both.

I would suggest that you pray and ask God for a freedom release in this area. When you are honest with God and admit that you need help in the area of tithes and offerings, He will begin the process in making sure you understand it with clarity, and that you will begin to have a heart to do so. It's okay, God loves when we ask Him for help. He rather we ask, than to not ask and act like we got this, when we don't, or we ask with the wrong heart intentions. God will reveal your heart even to yourself, so you will know what and how to ask Him for help.

> *Search me, O God, and know my heart: try me, and know my thoughts: And see if there be any wicked way in me, and lead me in the way everlasting. (Psalm 139:23–24, kjv)*

Ask, and it shall be given you; seek, and ye shall find; knock, and it shall be opened unto you: For every one that asketh receiveth; and he that seeketh findeth; and to him that knocketh it shall be opened. (Matthew 7:7–8, kjv)

Ye lust, and have not: ye kill, and desire to have, and cannot obtain: ye fight and war, yet ye have not, because ye ask not. Ye ask, and receive not, because ye ask amiss, that ye may consume it upon your lusts. (James 4:2–3, kjv)

God understands and knows we are all different and all of us have our own special areas of where we need help. Just because my area may not be tithes and offerings, there are other areas where I ask God for help. It is best not to hesitate in coming to God when you know you are struggling in a particular area. I love to pray and talk to God and I know He loves me coming to Him because we have a relationship and you can too, if you don't already. We should want to live a life where we are freely communicating with

God on a daily basis, this way we are open to hear and recognize more clearly when it is God's voice speaking to us. You will not know His voice if you are not communicating with Him on a regular basis. The same goes for when we work to build our other relationships, we begin to learn their likes and dislikes by spending time with them.

Learning the voice of God is the same, when you are reading His word and spending time in His presence through prayer and sitting quietly and allowing Him to speak to your heart and spirit, you will begin to learn and know His voice and His ways. This is why some believers may seem to grow faster than others in their relationship with the Lord; this is as a result of how much time each individual spends in getting to know God. Although, some may still question, but how do I know it is really the voice of God speaking to me? The number one way I would say you will know it is God; is by what you are hearing. Is what you are hearing lining up with the word of God? God will never go against or outside of His already written word, principles and guidelines. The only way to know what that written word is, is to pick up God's Word the Holy Bible and read it.

I am a huge believer on learning and knowing the word of God for yourself so that you are not falsely persuaded and lead astray. I encourage everyone to have their own personal time with the Lord and never solely rely on someone else's quality time they have spent in the word, or the experience and research of another person. It is each individual's own responsibility to seek after God and study the word for themselves. We can learn from one another, but you best be following it up with your own personal time. You can easily be persuaded in the wrong direction when you have not built a solid foundation with God on your own.

And ye shall seek me, and find me, when ye shall search for me with all your heart. (Jeremiah 29:13, kjv)

I love them that love me; and those that seek me early shall find me. (Proverbs 8:17, kjv)

Blessed are they which do hunger and thirst after righteousness: for they shall be filled. (Matthew 5:6, kjv)

For those who may not know or understand the importance of tithes and offerings, but desire to learn more and want to honor God in this area; I would say, pray and ask the Holy Spirit to make the word of God clear, so you will understand what God is speaking to you through His word as it relates to tithes and offerings. One thing God is not—He is not complicated. He is open and reveals His truths to anyone who wants to receive Him with a sincere heart.

As we grow in our relationship with God, we will begin to love what God loves and hate what God hates. In Proverbs 6:16–19, it states the six things that God hates and in Micah 6:8, it tells us clearly what the Lord requires of man to do. I would say this would be a great start in learning the heart of God and you will begin to recognize when it is God speaking to you. The Bible also speaks about God's love and how He wants the best for us; but you won't know His best nor have His best if you are not reading, studying and spending time with Him to learn His ways, His truths, and His voice.

These six things doth the Lord hate: yea, seven are an abomination unto him: A proud look, a lying tongue, and hands that shed innocent blood, An heart that deviseth wicked imaginations, feet that be swift in running to mischief, A false witness that speaketh lies, and he that soweth discord among brethren. (Proverbs 6:16–19, kjv)

He hath shewed thee, O man, what is good; and what doth the Lord require of thee, but to do justly, and to love mercy, and to walk humbly with thy God? (Micah 6:8, kjv)

Herein is love, not that we loved God, but that he loved us, and sent his Son to be the propitiation for our sins. (1 John 4:10, kjv)

For I the Lord thy God will hold thy right hand, saying unto thee, Fear not; I will help thee. (Isaiah 41:13, kjv)

CHAPTER 7

There Are No Self-Made Successes

In *Deuteronomy 8:18–20, kjv;* it states, *"it is he that giveth thee power to get wealth,"* Please know there is a freedom that comes when you are willing to be obedient to God as it relates to your giving. In your obedience to God's word, you will no doubt reap the benefits and blessings from God on a whole new level. You will be free to financially release what God is speaking to your heart to give.

This is just a thought, but maybe some are thinking they have achieved all of their accomplishments on their own. This could be a possible reason why they have a hard time in giving to God. Maybe they believe it was their wit, their smarts, their education, their know-how that got them to where they are and that it must be their own power that has gained their wealth; and for this reason, they should not have to share or give any of it to God or the Church. If by chance this is anybody's mind-set; please allow me to give you some help and let you know you can stop right there! Let me advise all, we wouldn't have the strength, the will, the power, the drive, the smarts, nor the determination or anything else, if it was not for the goodness of God giving us the life, the breath, the power, and the ability that graces us to do all that we do.

One phrase I have heard a lot and that is, "self-made" successes. Are you kidding me, did they create themselves? There is no person any-where that has created anything without God blessing them with the gift and talent to do so. It is God, and God alone, that has given each individual the smarts, the insight, the ability, and the God-given talent and gifts to accomplish any dream or goal we have set out to do. Never for-get God is the creator, author, and originator of all things; period, end of discussion. All we are and all we have all belongs to God; while we are living it is God's and when we die, we leave it behind. As I mentioned earlier, God wants us to be a good steward over what He has entrusted into our hands while we are living and what we do with what we have will show where our treasure lies; and where our treasure lies is where our heart will be and God wants our heart.

> *For by him were all things created, that are in heaven, and that are in earth, visible and invisible, whether they be thrones, or dominions, or principalities, or powers: all things were created by him, and for him: And he is before all things, and by him all things consist. (Colossians 1:16–17, kjv)*

> *But thou shalt remember the Lord thy God: for it is he that giveth thee power to get wealth, that he may establish his covenant which he sware unto thy fathers, as it is this day. (Deuteronomy 8:18, kjv)*

> *Thou art worthy, O Lord, to receive glory and honour and power: for thou hast created all things, and for thy pleasure they*

are and were created. (Revelation 4:11, kjv)

Know ye that the LORD he is God: it is he that hath made us, and not we ourselves; we are his people, and the sheep of his pasture. (Psalm 100:3, kjv)

And Jacob vowed a vow, saying, If God will be with me, and will keep me in this way that I go, and will give me bread to eat, and raiment to put on, So that I come again to my father's house in peace; then shall the LORD be my God: And this stone, which I have set for a pillar, shall be God's house: and of all that thou shalt give me I will surely give the tenth unto thee. (Genesis 28:20–22, kjv)

*Tithing isn't about taking
something from you;*

it's about getting something to you

*through your love and
obedience to GOD!*

ACKNOWLEDGEMENTS

First, I thank God for His goodness and mercies that are new every morning, and for His grace that is sufficient in every area of my life.

In loving memory, I give a special thank you to my parents, Ira E. and Doris C. Williams, who I continue to reap the overwhelming benefits from their gentle, yet strong and solid rearing; and to my brother, Tyrone, who will always hold a special place in my heart and who I miss every day.

To my husband and best friend, James, I love you and appreciate all your love, support, and encouragement; you inspire me when I need it most.

To my three sisters: Jan, thank you for your giving heart and service to the mission field; Sharon I appreciate your constant willingness to lend a helping hand; Carol, I value your humor and support that shows up at the right time.

In conclusion, I give a sincere thank you to all my family and friends who are special to me in their own way; you have blessed my life in ways you could never image.

ABOUT THE AUTHOR

Jacqui D. Williams-Skipwith was born in Washington D.C. She surrendered her life to Jesus Christ in the summer of 1974. Throughout the past forty-six years, she has served in several ministries and in 2001 completed a Minister's Internship Program. In 2018, she finished her first book—**"How Do I Know I Am Really Saved?"**, and is currently working on her third book—**"God Is Speaking to You"**. Jacqui is married, and presently lives in the Maryland area with her husband, James.

You may purchase Author's Books on:

Amazon, Barnes and Noble,
and Apple iTunes

View Author's Page on:

www.Amazon.com/author/jacquidwilliams

www.Goodreads.com

Your feedback is welcomed!